I0804087

Thank you for purchasing the Assimil e-course pack!

To download your e-course, just scan the QR code below and follow the instructions.

Or you can enter the following URL in your search engine:
monachat.assimil.online/livraison
Then enter the download code below and follow the instructions online.

YTwcbtjY

Note

To use the e-course on desktop or laptop computers:

- An internet connection is required
- The e-course can be installed on an unlimited number of devices, but only one can be active at a time

To use the e-course on tablets or smartphones:

- An internet connection is required for installation
- Utilisation is limited to three devices at a time
- On smartphones, portrait mode must be used

The guaranteed period of use is 36 months from the date of purchase. Thereafter, the application may no longer be usable if marketing or updates are discontinued.

In the following pages you'll find advice for getting the best out of your e-course. Feel free to contact us with any comments or questions at http://support.assimil.online/

Enjoy your language-learning experience!

The Assimil learning method, tried and proven for more than 90 years

The Assimil method was developed in 1929 by Alphonse Chérel, a globetrotting polyglot. He was early to realize that as travel became easier and more accessible to larger numbers of people, learning languages would become increasingly important.

He set out to develop a self-study course for French speakers to learn English: **L'anglais sans peine** (*English With Ease*). Soon, he added vinyl records with audio to support the lessons. This allowed learners to develop their oral alongside their reading and writing skills.

This first Assimil course was a huge success, and English was rapidly followed by other languages. Today, Assimil's catalogue includes courses allowing French speakers to learn more than 100 languages, as well as a range of courses for English-speaking learners.

The success of the Assimil method lies in its revolutionary pedagogy, which is based on the intuitive assimilation of a language. This is similar to the way we learn our first language as children: first by listening and understanding, then, little by little, beginning to voice words, then phrases, then sentences. This unique principle, which has allowed millions of learners to speak a new language, is delivered through around 100 lessons that gradually progress in difficulty.

The learning method consists of two key stages: the 'passive' phase

Collector's edition of **L'anglais sans peine** designed by the graphic designer and illustrator Noma Bar to commemorate Assimil's 85th anniversary

L'ITALIEN
SANS PEINE

and the 'active' phase.

The first stage (the first 50 lessons) focuses on the comprehension and assimilation of the language. The main goal is to try to understand what you read and hear. It is important to repeat each phrase aloud (with the aid of the phonetic transcriptions) to get used to pronouncing the language. Then read the translations and the notes, which explain key aspects of grammar or vocabulary.

The second stage, or the 'active phase', starts from lesson 50 on and involves studying a new lesson as before, but also going back to review a previous lesson, starting with lesson 1. This time, you translate the dialogues from English into the target language, allowing you to consolidate your learning and see how much progress you've made.

It goes without saying that Assimil courses have dramatically evolved over the last 90 years, ultimately leading to the digital version you will be using. However, its core principles have remained the same. Why change a winning formula?

How to get the best out of this course
The 10 essentials

1 **Start with a positive attitude and have confidence in yourself.** The language you want to learn isn't difficult. The hardest language to learn is always your first: your mother tongue.

2 **Repeat each line of the dialogue and exercises aloud.** It's important to practice speaking right from the start.

3 **Follow the order of the lessons.** Don't try to run before you can walk!

4 **Do the exercises.** Even if they seem easy, they allow you to put into practice what you've just learned.

5 **Don't skip the review lessons.** These are crucial for recall and to consolidate your learning.

6 **Study regularly.** Learning a language is no different than learning anything else: it requires diligent, regular practice.

7 **Quality is better than quantity.** Try to make time to study for 20–30 minutes a day: the key to learning is consistency and concentration, not the amount you fit into one session.

8 **Don't get discouraged!** When you least expect it, you'll realize how much progress you've made!

9 **Don't be shy.** It doesn't matter if you make mistakes. Just keep expressing yourself: practice makes perfect.

10 **Keep practicing.** Listening, reading, writing and speaking as often as possible will ensure your level continues to improve.

To find out how to use your e-course, a video is worth a thousand words

That's why we've created a tutorial. Just scan the QR code below with your smartphone or tablet to access it.

The e-course allows you to:

1. Listen to the dialogues of the lessons as many times as you wish.
2. Display the phonetic transcriptions and/or word stress.
3. Record yourself speaking and compare your pronunciation with that of native speakers as many times as you need to.
4. Complete multiple-choice questions to check your language comprehension.
5. Do the exercises to consolidate your learning by reconstructing sentences.
6. Self-assess your progress.

To watch the tutorial, scan the QR code with your smartphone or tablet. You can also watch the video on Assimil's YouTube channel.

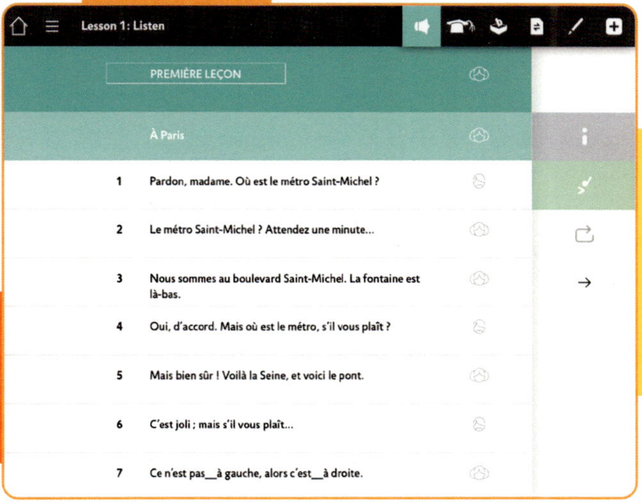
Lesson 1: Listen
PREMIÈRE LEÇON
À Paris
1 Pardon, madame. Où est le métro Saint-Michel ?
2 Le métro Saint-Michel ? Attendez une minute…
3 Nous sommes au boulevard Saint-Michel. La fontaine est là-bas.
4 Oui, d'accord. Mais où est le métro, s'il vous plaît ?
5 Mais bien sûr ! Voilà la Seine, et voici le pont.
6 C'est joli ; mais s'il vous plaît…
7 Ce n'est pas__à gauche, alors c'est__à droite.

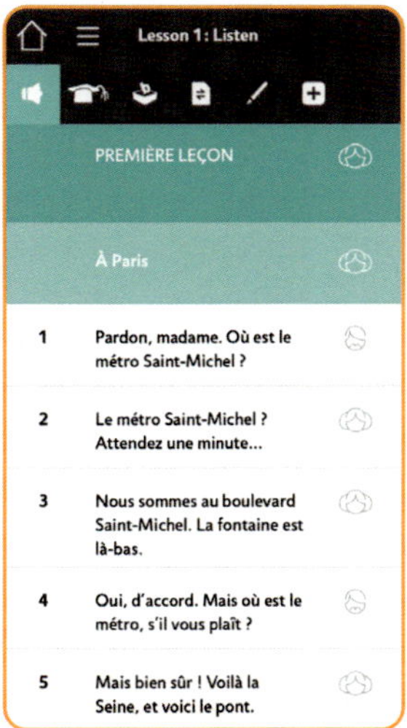
Lesson 1: Listen
PREMIÈRE LEÇON
À Paris
1 Pardon, madame. Où est le métro Saint-Michel ?
2 Le métro Saint-Michel ? Attendez une minute…
3 Nous sommes au boulevard Saint-Michel. La fontaine est là-bas.
4 Oui, d'accord. Mais où est le métro, s'il vous plaît ?
5 Mais bien sûr ! Voilà la Seine, et voici le pont.

French
published by Assimil

Französisch lernen
Learn French
Aprender Francés
Frans Leren
Fransızca Öğrenmek
Изучение французского языка